WORLD'S DEADLIEST REPTILES

Thanks to the creative team:
Senior Editor: Alice Peebles
Fact checking: Tim Harris
Designer: www.mayermedia.co.uk

Hungry Tomato®
A division of Lerner Publishing Group, Inc.
241 First Avenue North
Minneapolis, MN 55401 USA

For reading levels and more information, look up
this title at www.lernerbooks.com.

Main body text set in Calisto MT 12.5/14.5.
Typeface provided by Monotype Typography.

Library of Congress Cataloging-in-Publication Data

Names: Jackson, Tom, 1972– author. | Jevtic, Vladimir,
illustrator.
Title: World's deadliest reptiles / Tom Jackson ; [illustrator]
Vladimir Jevtic.
Description: Minneapolis : Hungry Tomato, [2018] | Series:
Extreme reptiles | Audience: Ages 8-12. | Audience: Grades
4 to 6. | Includes index. | Identifiers: LCCN 2018004244
(print) | LCCN 2018005565 (ebook) | ISBN 9781541523869
(eb pdf) | ISBN 9781541500907 (lb : alk. paper)
Subjects: LCSH: Dangerous reptiles—Juvenile literature. |
Reptiles—Miscellanea—Juvenile literature.
Classification: LCC QL645.7 (ebook) | LCC QL645.7 .J33
2018 (print) | DDC 597.9165—dc23

LC record available at https://lccn.loc.gov/2018004244

Manufactured in the United States of America
1-43759-33619-3/27/2018

WORLD'S
DEADLIEST
REPTILES

by Tom Jackson
Illustrated by Vladimir Jevtic

HUNGRY
TOMATO®
Minneapolis

CONTENTS

DEADLY REPTILES

There are 10,000 reptile species on Earth. Most are completely harmless and some even make good pets. However, several reptiles are highly dangerous. It is thought that more than 90,000 people die every year because of deadly reptiles! We should remember, though, that most of these reptiles are not looking for humans to kill. Often the killer creatures give us a clear warning before attacking, and they will only use their deadly defenses when they feel that they have no other way to escape.

This African bush viper is about to strike.

A Nile crocodile has grabbed an impala, an African antelope.

PUMPING POISON

A deadly reptile's powerful defenses come from its extreme hunting skills. Reptile hunters use strength, speed, and stealth, but they are also the masters of another weapon: venom. Venom is a poison that attacks the body of a victim, making it too weak to fight back. (Often prey are eaten while still alive—just barely!) Other animals and plants might be poisonous and make animals sick if they eat them, but they are not using venom. A venom has to be injected into the target animal's body by the attacker. The most powerful reptile venom is created by snakes, which have needle-shaped fangs for pumping it out during a deep bite. There are a few lizards that use venom as well.

Snake fangs have pipes and grooves for channeling venom.

A tree snake clings to its meal—it cannot let go!

DEATH CRUSH

The other way that reptiles kill is by using great strength. Big reptiles like crocodiles and pythons are among the strongest animals on the planet. Once they have a victim in their grasp, there is no escape, and death is moments away. Turtles are a largely slow-moving and harmless group of reptiles. However, like their more deadly cousins, turtles can give very damaging bites. Deadly reptiles are beautiful but dangerous, and as with all wildlife, it is always better to simply watch them from a safe distance.

HOODS AND HISSES

A cobra knows how to give another animal a fright. It raises its head above the ground and folds out its rib bones to transform its head into a dark hood.

The back of the hood has dark spots connected with a pale loop. This makes the cobra's hood look like the face of a much larger—and stronger—creature.

Cobras are very shy and, if they are disturbed, prefer to slither out of sight if they can. They spend most of their time curled up in a dark burrow, and come out to hunt at night.

Some African cobras will attack a dangerous animal, such as this mongoose, before it gets within biting distance. The snake spits stinging venom in its eyes.

Snake charmers play a trick. The snake is kept in a dark basket and rises up when the lid is taken off. The snake thinks the flute is another snake, and follows it from side to side as the charmer sways it.

COBRAS
NAJA SPECIES
Lifespan: 20 years
Size: 10 feet (3.1 m)

COBRAS

Cobras are highly venomous snakes from Asia and Africa. They are probably the scariest snakes of all and are famous for their wide, hooded necks. People really should be scared of them. The Indian cobra bites 250,000 people every year and about 50,000 of them die before they can get treatment. However, cobras do not want to attack people—that is why they put on such a show to scare us away!

NERVE POISON
Cobra venom contains chemicals that attack the nerves. This makes a victim's muscles stop working, and they eventually die because they are unable to breathe in and out.

WIDE VARIETY
There are more than 30 species of cobra. They live in forests, swamps and rivers, and on farmland, hunting for mice, frogs, lizards, and fish.

Dark Warnings

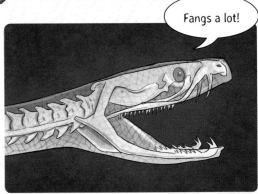

The black mamba holds the snake speed record: 12 mph (20 km/h), so an Olympic sprinter could get away—unless the slithering snake is hidden in grass.

As with other venomous snakes, the fangs fold up against the roof of the mouth and only fold down to bite. They are hollow to channel venom into prey.

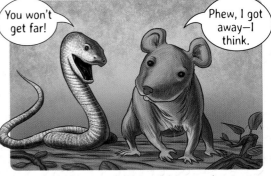

Black mambas hunt during the day. They may use their speed to chase down prey, but usually hide and wait for prey to pass by. They mostly eat small mammals, but also attack birds and other snakes.

The snake has powerful venom that attacks a victim's heart and muscles. It can take a minute or two to have its deadly effect. The snake lets its prey go, and waits . . .

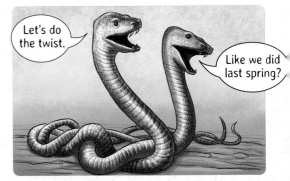

The mamba follows the dying prey, and once it collapses, the snake swallows it whole, head first. The mamba has very powerful stomach juices. This meal will be completely digested in under 10 hours.

In spring, female mambas attract males with scent. If two males turn up, they fight. They coil around each other and raise their heads high in shows of strength. The winner pins the loser to the ground.

BLACK MAMBA

The black mamba is Africa's deadliest snake—its bite is called the "kiss of death." The snake's venom is so strong that a mamba bite is nearly always deadly. Anyone bitten needs to get to hospital fast. That is not always easy because the venom will make them unconscious in 45 minutes— and die a few hours later.

BLACK MAMBA
DENDROASPIS POLYLEPIS
Lifespan: 11 years
Size: 9 feet 10 inches (3 m)

SMILING SNAKE
Mambas have a rectangular head, which is sometimes called coffin-shaped. The long mouth seems to smile at you. Don't be fooled.

LONG AND DANGEROUS
The black mamba is the longest venomous snake in Africa, and the second longest in the world, after the king cobra of Asia.

GAPING MOUTH
A black mamba is not black, but more of a pale gray-brown color. However, when it opens its mouth to warn off an attacker, it reveals menacin black gums and long fangs. This is where it gets it name.

HERE BE DRAGONS

Komodo dragons spend most of their time alone. When another dragon comes into their area, there will be a fight. Wrestling on their back legs, they use their clawed front feet to slash at their rival.

The huge lizards have to sunbathe for hours each day to warm up their bodies. Once they are nice and warm, they can run as fast a person—for a short distance—to catch their prey.

They produce a lot of thick, sticky saliva that contains a slow-acting poison. This stops their bite from healing, so prey continues to bleed until it dies.

The venom takes days to kill large prey, so the lizard just follows it around until it falls down dead. The dragon tracks the smell with its forked tongue.

Dragons also eat carrion: the flesh of already dead animals. They can sniff out a dead body from more than 5 miles (8 km) away. Several dragons will feast on a large animal like a buffalo.

KOMODO DRAGON

The island of Komodo in the South Pacific is home to dragons. The Komodo dragon is the world's largest lizard. It looks like a regular lizard with scaly skin, a forked tongue, short, waddling legs, and a long, swishing tail—but it is the length of a rhinoceros. The dragons are the largest hunters anywhere on the island. They prey on any animal they can find, from birds and smaller lizards to wild pigs and buffalo—and any people who come too close.

KOMODO DRAGON
VARANUS KOMODOENSIS
Lifespan: 30 years
Size: 10 feet (3.1 m)

BABY DANGER
Adult dragons will eat their babies if they can. The young dragons are small and agile enough to climb, so they hide in the branches out of the way of lumbering monsters on the ground.

SOLE SURVIVORS
There used to be giant, flesh-eating lizards like this across what is now Indonesia and Australia. Those monster reptiles are extinct now, and Komodo Island's lizards are the only dragons left.

WATER MONSTER

A crocodile could not catch a zebra on land—the zebra is much faster at running. However, in water, the croc usually wins. It approaches silently with just its eyes and nostrils above the water, so the zebra does not see it approaching.

Nile crocodiles strike with lightning speed, lurching out of the water to grab prey. This croc has the strongest bite of any living animal. It grips its prey with a force of 5,000 lb./in.^{2} (350 kg/cm^2). That is enough to crack concrete.

Despite having mighty jaws, a crocodile cannot bite off a mouthful of flesh very easily. It has to twist its body around to rip out a chunk.

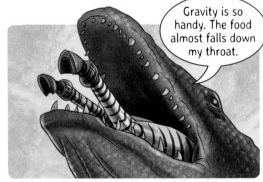

The crocodile crushes smaller prey in its jaws, but uses the water to kill larger animals. The zebra is pulled down deep and held there until it drowns.

It cannot chew well, either. Instead it swallows everything in big chunks. It lifts up its head and chugs food down its wide throat all in one go.

NILE CROCODILE

Nile crocodiles are the largest reptiles in Africa, and they live all over the continent, not just in the River Nile. Crocodiles have been hunting in rivers for at least 80 million years. Back then they were attacking dinosaurs that came to the waterside to drink. The crocodile hunting system is so good that they have just kept on doing it ever since. Nile crocs are not fussy eaters. They snap up fish, mammals, birds, and turtles—and also eat about 500 people a year.

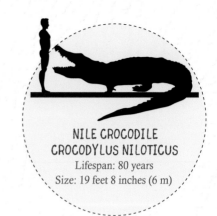

NILE CROCODILE
CROCODYLUS NILOTICUS
Lifespan: 80 years
Size: 19 feet 8 inches (6 m)

ARMORED SKIN
The crocodile has plates of bones under its skin called scutes. The scutes form armored ridges along its back and tail.

LURKING BENEATH
A Nile crocodile can dive under the water for 30 minutes at a time. Even if the river looks empty, there may be a croc lurking just out of sight.

BIG MOUTH

The world's longest snake is the reticulated python of southern Asia. A full-sized adult can grow to 20 feet (6 m) long if it gets plenty of food. However, unlike other animals, snakes never stop growing. On rare occasions pythons have reached 33 feet (10 m) long.

You're hot!

Pythons have a super sense for tracking prey. Small pits on the snout are sensitive to the heat given off by other animals. The python can pick up this heat even if prey is hidden behind a bush in the night!

Let me hold you tighter.

Pythons are ambush hunters. They wait for prey to come close, throw their body around it, and squeeze, tightening a little more each time its victim breathes out. Eventually, it cannot breathe at all—and dies.

I can swallow almost any animal, but it takes me about an hour.

The snake swallows prey head first, so the limbs fold down flat. Its lower jaw is in two halves and can spread sideways. It also hangs from the skull on stretchy skin so the mouth opens really wide.

Yawn, I normally sleep for a couple of months after a big meal!

The python has many hooked teeth. As well as giving a nasty bite, they enable the snake to haul itself around its food. The meal does not really go into the snake—the snake goes around the meal!

PYTHONS

Pythons are among the longest snakes in the world. They do not kill prey with a venomous bite. Instead, they are constrictors, using their size and strength to crush the life out of their victims. These big snakes live all over Africa, Asia, and Australia, and there are not many animals that are safe from a python's deadly cuddle. These snakes stay away from big hunting cats like tigers and leopards—but will eat their cubs given the chance.

RETICULATED PYTHON
PYTHON RETICULATUS
Lifespan: 20 years
Size: 21 feet 3 inches (6.5 m)

MEASURE UP
A python can kill a big animal, but will not bother unless it looks small enough to swallow. Greedy pythons have been known to burst open after eating meals that are just too big.

COMING FOR DINNER
Pythons seldom eat humans, but in remote jungle areas of Southeast Asia, giant reticulated pythons sometimes slide into homes at night and attack people as they sleep. Nearly always, the human victims can raise the alarm and are rescued.

SNAKES OF THE SEA

Land snakes lie flat on their bellies so they can slide along. Sea snakes are almost round, but their tails are flattened into a paddle shape. They still swim with a curving, side-to-side movement.

The banded sea krait lives in coral reefs and hunts moray eels, which can be just as fierce. Eels pretend to be snakes to scare away predators. The snake pretends to be an eel to get close enough to attack.

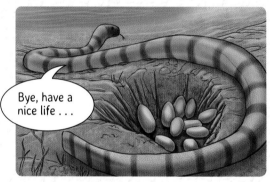

Sea kraits are the only sea snakes to come on land. They need to find somewhere dry to lay their eggs, and they slip into beachside caves to make nests. Mothers leave the eggs and never see their young.

The yellow-bellied sea snake spends its whole life at sea. It is a strong swimmer but is too weak and floppy to move on land. It uses its highly toxic venom to kill fish in seconds before they can swim away.

Yellow-bellied sea snakes give birth to their babies, rather than laying eggs. The tiny snakes cannot swim far and spend their early years on seaweed floating at the surface. Little fish come to shelter under the seaweed and nibble on it. The little snakes dive in and snatch them.

SEA SNAKES

Coral reefs are beautiful places, filled with colorful wildlife. But watch out: there are even snakes here—and they are among the deadliest in the world. Sea snakes spend most of their time underwater. They have to come to the surface for a breath of fresh air, but they can then stay under for more than than two hours—and dive down as far as 330 feet (100 m) beneath the surface.

SEA SNAKES
HYDROPHIINAE SPECIES
Lifespan: 10 years
Size: 9 feet 10 inches (3 m)

FRESH DRINK

Sea snakes cannot drink seawater because it is too salty for them. They can go for several months without a drink. During heavy rain, the snakes swim to the surface where fresh, unsalted water forms in small pools for a few minutes before mixing in with the seawater.

LONG LUNG

Being long and narrow, snakes have one main lung—the other is very small. Sea snakes have a lung that runs the whole length of the body, so they can take big breaths.

THE FIERCE SNAKE

The inland taipan is also called "the fierce snake" because it can defend itself spectacularly. Hissing, it lifts up the front half of its sturdy body in a tight "S" shape. If not left alone, it will straighten its body, lunge forward, and bite in a tiny fraction of second.

In summer, the taipan is a pale green-yellow. Heat reflects off its body, stopping it from getting too hot. In winter, the desert can get chilly, so the taipan's color shifts to a darker brown to absorb more heat. This keeps the snake active in the cold.

Inland taipans live in very remote, semi-arid areas of central Australia. They are very shy, spending weeks at a time resting under shady rocks. In fact, no specimens were found between 1882 and 1972, when they were rediscovered. Despite this, they are not considered in danger of extinction.

A taipan's venom is a killer cocktail. It contains chemicals that attack the brain, cause internal bleeding, make muscles twitch, and stop the kidneys from working. The poisons in one bite from a taipan are enough to kill 100 fully grown men. Within an hour, most would become paralyzed and then be unable to breathe.

INLAND TAIPAN

The inland taipan lives in the deserts of Australia. It is a shy snake and is seldom seen. It spends most of the day staying cool in a burrow under rocks. At night it slides out to look for prey. It only ever eats small mammals such as rats and mice. There is not much food in a desert, so when the taipan does find a meal it makes sure its prize does not escape—and it does this with the most powerful venom of any snake.

INLAND TAIPAN
OXYURANUS SPECIES
Lifespan: 20 years
Size: 8 feet (2.5 m)

KILLER BITES
When threatened, most snakes give dry bites at first. This means they inject no venom, or only a little. Their venom is valuable stuff. However, taipans always give wet bites. They always bite to kill.

SAFE BUT DEADLY
Despite its very powerful venom, no one has died from a taipan bite in the last 100 years. Wild snakes nearly always slither away when people get near. When a snake collector gets bitten by their pet taipan, they know to go straight to hospital.

GRISLY GATOR

Spot the difference!

Snap!

Stay cool, kids.

Alligators and crocodiles are similar but different. A gator has a wider, shorter snout for snapping up smaller prey. When its mouth is shut, it only shows its upper teeth. A croc shows its lower teeth as well.

Alligators bask on the bank to warm up in the sunshine. When they get too hot, they swing open their huge jaws to lose heat from their moist mouth. They have strong muscles for biting down on prey.

It's my mudhole, and I dig it.

I'm just pretending to be a pile of old sticks.

In summer, the swamp dries out, so an alligator digs itself a mudhole. This traps a small pool for the gator to bathe in until rains refill the swamp.

Alligators are cunning, and among the few animals that use tools. Researchers have seen how they trick birds into coming close so they can be grabbed.

Don't mind me. I'm just a talking log.

Erm, excuse me, I need to build a nest.

The alligator has balanced some twigs on its snout. This is nesting time for birds and the twigs will make good building materials.

The alligator's eyes swivel sideways so it can see the bird approaching. As soon as the bird is close enough, the gator snaps it up in one great gulp.

AMERICAN ALLIGATORS

Alligators are swamp-loving killer creatures. While not as big as crocodiles, they are the top predators in America's Deep South. From North Carolina to the southern coast of Texas, any water deeper than chest height could contain a hungry gator. Alligators eat fish, frogs, crabs, and waterbirds, and they sometimes come on land on warm nights to snap up mammals, such as rats and raccoons.

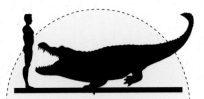

AMERICAN ALLIGATOR
ALLIGATOR MISSISSIPPIENSIS
Lifespan: 50 years
Size: 14 feet 9 inches (4.5 m)

CHINESE COUSIN
Alligators are famous American animals. However, they also have relatives that live in the swamps of China. The Chinese alligators are smaller than American ones and much rarer.

MAN EATERS
Most alligators see humans as being just too big to eat. However, about five Americans get bitten by gators every year, although they normally escape alive. As more people set up homes in waterside communities, attacks could become more of a problem.

AMBUSH SNAPPER

Alligator snapping turtles hang out on the muddy riverbed. They go to the surface to breathe every 40 minutes or so, but otherwise lie still on the bottom with their mouth open. But what's that?

The red "worm" is part of the turtle's tongue. It wiggles in the murky water, catching the eye of hungry fish swimming past. Sooner or later, a fish swims over to take a nibble.

Snap! The fish is the turtle's next meal. Despite its tough, armored body, the turtle has a long, flexible neck to help it snatch fish in a flash. At night, turtles patrol the river looking for extra tidbits.

Alligator snapping turtles get their name from their ridged shell and long spiked tail, which makes them look like a little alligator wearing a suit of armor. They will eat baby alligators but leave adults alone.

The alligator snapping turtle is the largest freshwater turtle in the world. Sea turtles are generally larger, as are the giant land tortoises found on a few ocean islands.

ALLIGATOR SNAPPING TURTLE

The alligator snapping turtle lives in the rivers and backwaters of the southeastern United States. They stay far out in deep water most of the time and only occasionally come on land. The females emerge to lay their eggs in a nest on the bank. The bigger males only come out if their home has dried out and they need to search out another. Leave the big ugly beasts alone—their bite can take a finger clean off.

ALLIGATOR SNAPPING TURTLE
MACROCHELYS TEMMINCKII
Lifespan: up to 70 years
Size: 3 feet 3 inches (1 m)

CRACKING JOB
Alligator snapping turtles mainly eat fish and shellfish. They also prey on smaller river turtles. The snappers crack open their victims' shells with their sharp hooked beaks.

OLD TIMERS
It is thought that alligator snapping turtles could live up to 200 years, making them the oldest American animals. The turtles keep growing very slowly all their lives, and some very old specimens weigh more than 220 pounds (100 kg). However, most snapping turtles are thought to live to about 70 years old.

TERRIFYING RASP

Saw-scaled snakes are tiny compared to other deadly snakes. Some African species are barely longer than a man's foot. The little snakes hunt for little prey, such as scorpions, frogs, and insects.

The snakes are named after their rough scales. Each scale has a ridge, or keel, down the middle. The top of each keel has a saw-tooth shape, so the snake feels very rough—if you're silly enough to touch it!

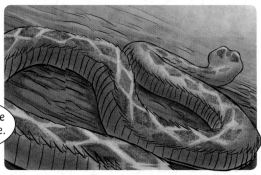

The snake makes a loud, terrifying noise with its "saw" scales to scare people off. It curls its body into a thick U-shape, and rubs its scales together. The high-pitched rasping sounds a bit like food. sizzling.

The snake's loud warning does not last long. It is quick to strike, unleashing probably the fastest bite of any snake, as it jumps forward in less than the blink of an eye.

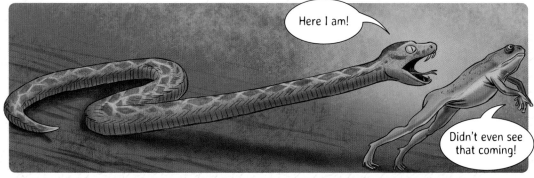

The little snake hurls itself at its target with such force that it sometimes takes off and flies through the air. Ancient people sometimes talked of "fiery flying serpents," and it is suggested that the reddish, flame-colored vipers of the Middle East may be what they were talking about.

SAW-SCALED VIPERS

The saw-scaled vipers live in desert areas of Africa and southern Asia. They are small snakes but make up for that with a terrifying display that warns other animals to stay away. Saw-scaled vipers are the most aggressive snakes in the world. Most snakes will always slither away from trouble if they can. These deadly little vipers not only stand their ground, but bite fast and bite often!

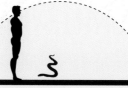

SAW-SCALED VIPERS
ECHIS SPECIES
Lifespan: 20 years
Size: 35 inches (90 cm)

UPS AND DOWNS
The snake normally spends the day lurking under rocks and logs and comes out at night. During periods of rain, the snakes climb into bushes to hunt—and perhaps keep clear of the puddles collecting in their usual hiding places.

DANGEROUS TO KNOW
The venom of a saw-scaled viper is not as powerful as that of many other snakes, but this snake bites people so often that it is still one of the world's most dangerous types.

MORE DEADLY REPTILES

The world's deadliest reptiles are mostly living in Southeast Asia and Australia. The demands on their survival have made them deadlier than reptiles elsewhere. Every continent has dangerous reptiles. So watch out wherever you are.

Fer-de-lance: Also known as the terciopelo, this viper from the rainforest of Central and South America uses a venom that keeps working for weeks after a bite, eating away at the victim's flesh. The snake often turns to flee a threat, only to suddenly swing around again and deliver a bite.

Mexican beaded lizard: At 32 inches (80 cm) long, this is the largest lizard in North America. The lumbering creature lives in the deserts of southern Mexico. It is one of the very few lizards that produce venom. It does not have fangs like a snake and so mixes its poison into its victim's blood by chewing on them. The venom is a nerve poison. It makes the lizard's bite hurt a lot, but no one has ever died from a beaded lizard attack.

Tree crocodile: Also called the crocodile monitor, this lizard is a smaller relative of the Komodo dragon—and is only distantly related to actual crocodiles. It is black with yellow-green speckles and has a long croc-shaped body. Instead of swimming, the 198-pound (90-kg), 10-foot (3-m) beast lives mostly in trees, using its speed and long, toothy jaws to snatch prey. If threatened by a human, it leaps down from the branches and gives a nasty bite. The lizard's saliva is filled with bacteria that make the wound dangerously infected.

Adder: Although not very deadly compared to many other snakes, the adder is the only venomous snake in many parts of the world. The adder is also the most widespread snake of all. It is found as far west as Britain and as far east as North Korea, and lives further north than any other snake. The snakes in colder areas are almost black so they can absorb heat. An adder's venom is very weak, but people who are bitten should check with a doctor.

AMAZING REPTILE FACTS

Even after a snake's head has been chopped off, it can still be deadly. The snake's brain will stay alive for several hours, and the fangs bite down on anything that touches them—making a real-life horror show! Even when a snake looks dead, you should be careful about touching it.

Crocodiles cry as they eat a large meal. The tears flow not because the monster is feeling sorry for its victim, but because the croc gulps in air as it eats. As it pushes the air out in big puffs, the air presses on the tear glands (which are there for washing the eyes) and makes it cry.

Snakes cannot blink because they have no eyelids. Instead they have a transparent scale over the eye to protect it and keep it clean—and they sleep with their eyes wide open. Even when snoozing, deadly snakes are on the lookout for something to kill!

Snakes, such as rattlers and cottonmouths, are the second most dangerous animals in the United States. They kill more people than mountain lions, wolves, and alligators. Only bears are more deadly.

GLOSSARY

antivenin a medicine used to stop the damaging effects of a snake's venom

backwater a dead-end stretch of water that is fed by a larger river, making a quiet area of still water

constrictor a snake that kills by squeezing its prey

continent a large section of Earth's land. Earth has seven continents: Africa, Antarctica, Asia, Australia, Europe, North America, and South America.

gravity the force that pulls everything down to the ground

mammal an animal that feeds its young on milk; nearly all mammals also have hairy bodies. A human is a mammal.

paralyzed unable to move because the muscles or nerves are not working

prey the animals eaten by a hunter

rasping a sound made by rubbing rough surfaces together

reticulated having a net shape or pattern

saliva another word for spit

serpent an old-fashioned word for snake

toxic another word for poisonous

venom a poison produced by an animal that is pumped into prey or an attacker to kill them

INDEX

The Author
Tom Jackson has written about 200 books over 25 years—his specialties are natural history, technology, and all things scientific. Tom studied zoology at Bristol University and has worked in zoos and as a conservationist. He's mucked out polar bears, surveyed in the Vietnamese jungle, and rescued wildlife from drought in Africa. Writing jobs have also taken him to the Galápagos Islands, the Amazon rainforest, and the Sahara. Today, Tom lives in Bristol, England, with his wife and three children, and can be found mostly in the attic.

The Illustrator
Vladimir Jevtic was born and lives in the Republic of Serbia. In 2015, he graduated in illustration and book design from the Faculty of Applied Arts at Belgrade's University of Arts. He followed up with a Master's in academic studies in 2016. During these years, Vladimir drew caricatures and illustrations for the popular Serbian weekly magazine *Politikin Zabavnik*. He has also illustrated the children's books *You Can't Go In* (2016) and *Ola the Ostrich* (2017).

Picture Credits (abbreviations: t = top; b = bottom; c = center; l = left; r = right)
© www.shutterstock.com:

1 c, 2 cl, 3 c, 4 c, 5 b, 6 tl, 6 b, 7 tr, 7 bl, 9 c, 11 c, 13 c, 15 c, 19 c, 21 c, 23 c, 25 c, 27 c, 28 tr, 28 bl, 29 tr, 29 b, 31 cr, 32r.

Every effort has been made to trace the copyright holders, and we acknowledge in advance for any unintentional omissions. We would be pleased to insert the appropriate acknowledgements in any subsequent edition of this publication.